THE REAL SCIENCE OF
MIND CONTROL

Corey Anderson

Lerner Publications ◆ Minneapolis

Lerner Publications Company
An imprint of Lerner Publishing Group, Inc.
241 First Avenue North
Minneapolis, MN 55401 USA

For reading levels and more information, look up this title at www.lernerbooks.com.

Library of Congress Cataloging-in-Publication Data

Names: Anderson, Corey, author.
Title: The real science of mind control / Corey Anderson.
Description: Minneapolis : Lerner Publications, [2022] | Series: The real science of superpowers (Alternator books) | Includes bibliographical references and index. | Audience: Ages 8–12 | Audience: Grades 4–6 | Summary: "In the hands of a supervillain, mind control is a nightmare. But in real life, doctors and scientists control the mind to help patients and improve people's lives"— Provided by publisher.
Identifiers: LCCN 2021018531 (print) | LCCN 2021018532 (ebook) | ISBN 9781728441252 (library binding) | ISBN 9781728449586 (paperback) | ISBN 9781728445311 (ebook)
Subjects: LCSH: Control (Psychology)—Juvenile literature. | Mental suggestion—Juvenile literature. | Brainwashing—Juvenile literature.
Classification: LCC BF632.5 A56 2022 (print) | LCC BF632.5 (ebook) | DDC 153.8/53—dc23

LC record available at https://lccn.loc.gov/2021018531
LC ebook record available at https://lccn.loc.gov/2021018532

Manufactured in the United States of America
1-49896-49739-7/1/2021

TABLE OF CONTENTS

In stories, heroes sometimes uncover the truth by reading a suspect's mind.

You're in a police station, sitting across from a handcuffed suspect. The police think he stole a famous piece of art, but he won't say where he hid it. You're there to help. You have a special superpower.

You look into the suspect's eyes and concentrate. The suspect's mind is under your control. You make him tell the truth about where he hid the painting. The police go to that location and recover the art. You are a hero!

This kind of complete mind control only happens in comic books and movies. In reality, there are some ways to influence the way a person acts or speaks. But we cannot directly control someone else's independent thoughts and words.

Controlling machines with our minds, though, is becoming a real possibility. Imagine sending a text message without picking up a phone. You could hop in a car and drive to your destination by just thinking of where you want to go. Scientists and technologists are creating these advancements right now. This is our future.

In the future, people may be able to control cars with their thoughts.

CHAPTER 1

CONTROLLING THE MIND

Mind control is a way for fictional heroes to overcome bad guys.

Mind control is the ability for people to control technology with their minds. It can also be the ability to influence the thoughts and actions of others. Mind control can be used to sway people to speak or do things differently than they normally would. Sometimes, it is used for fun. Other times, it is used to harm people.

Guided hypnotism is a type of mind control. A hypnotist uses relaxation and focusing techniques to put a human subject in a trancelike state. A trance is a condition in which a person is not fully conscious, but still in control of their own actions. They are easily influenced by the suggestions of the hypnotist. For instance, if a hypnotist suggests the room is very cold, the hypnotized person will feel an extreme chill. Guided hypnotism can be fun. It can make people do silly things. Sometimes it is used as therapy. It helps people break bad habits, like chewing their nails.

Hypnosis is also seen in comic books and science fiction stories. Bad guys might use it to rob a bank. They could hypnotize the bank workers and tell them to open a safe full of money.

Hypnosis might help someone change an unwanted habit, like nail-biting.

Another form of mind control is brainwashing. Brainwashing is when a person's thoughts or actions are manipulated against their will. Unlike a hypnotist, the brainwasher is often in total control of the person being brainwashed. They might control things like the person's sleep, what they eat, and the information that they have access to. This control takes away the brainwashed person's ability to think independently. A brainwashed person might say or do things they might not have thought or done on their own.

A brainwasher might control every aspect of a person's life.

#1. $(7 \times 39) + (3 \times 1) =$?

#5.

#2. $(9 \times 1? \quad 25) =$?

A

#3. $(60 \div 5$

Sometimes people use mind control on themselves. The power of suggestion is a way to influence the mind. Just thinking a certain way about something can affect the results. For example, if you think you are going to fail an upcoming math test, then it's more likely you will do poorly. If you expect you will do well, that confidence may help.

CHAPTER 2
MEGA MIND POWER

Many characters in stories and movies use mind control to get their way.

Mind control is one of the most common superpowers in comic books, video games, and science fiction stories. Some characters can put themselves in a trance to concentrate their power. Other times, they can make characters fall asleep or control characters' minds. They might be able to control characters from far away, or they might have to touch them. This is called tactile mind control.

The mind control and hypnosis in comic books and science fiction is not possible in real life. Nobody's mind is powerful enough to overcome someone else's.

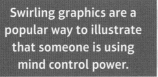

Swirling graphics are a popular way to illustrate that someone is using mind control power.

Mind control is a power seen in movies too. Fantasy worlds have magicians who cast mind-control spells and curses. Their spells can be used for both good and evil.

In science fiction movies, some characters have special physical and mental abilities. They use mind tricks to get their way. Gestures and voice tones hypnotize other characters. But these mind tricks only work on characters with weak minds.

Wizards use spells to control the minds of others in some popular stories. Some can do it from far away.

A character locked up in a dungeon could use mind control to convince a weak-minded guard to let them go. Or they could convince a crowd of people to help them tear down the dungeon walls.

Writers and directors use mind control as a plot device to make exciting things happen in stories.

SUPERFAST FACT

When you are awake, your brain makes enough electricity to power a light bulb.

Fictional spies can use mind control to get what they want. Secret agents use a truth liquid, or serum, to learn things villains may be hiding. Sometimes, the serum is injected like a shot. Other times, spies in fantasy stories sneak it into a drink. Then they wait for the villain to start talking. Evildoers might not know they're spilling their secrets, even as they're doing it.

Mind control could be used to save the day. It could also be a dangerous tool. Criminals could learn where people keep their most valuable possessions and steal them.

Everyone has secrets. With mind control, you might learn every secret a person has. Knowing every minor detail about someone might make you think differently about them, even a close friend or family member.

In movies, evildoers sometimes inject truth serum to get heroes to reveal secrets.

AMAZING ANIMAL POWER

A parasite with mind control powers lives inside of mice. The parasite causes the mouse to lose its fear of cats! It wants a cat to eat the mouse so the parasite can live inside the cat. Then the parasite ends up in the cat's poop. A new mouse nibbles on the poop, starting the cycle over again.

Some mice carry parasites that alter their minds.

CHAPTER 3
MODERN MIND CONTROL

Thanks to medical technology, doctors have the ability to observe the electrical activity of a person's mind.

lthough the mind-reading techniques often seen in movies aren't real, mind-reading technology can help scientists and doctors understand people and patients better. Special machines monitor electrical activity in the brain. For instance, if a person is thinking of something that makes them angry, electrical activity occurs in certain parts of their brains. The machine can monitor and record that activity.

Some people worry about the possibility of mind-reading technology going too far. What happens if we can read more than emotion? For instance, what if a person thought about committing a crime? Should law enforcement officials try to prevent a person from committing a crime that they had only thought about?

Using mind control to prevent crime could violate people's rights.

Brain-scanning machines can help doctors find previously unknown medical conditions before they happen. They might figure out whether a person's brain will be able to learn something easily or not. A doctor might discover that a young child will have trouble learning to read. Parents and teachers can start helping that child right away. Other conditions, like attention disorders or depression, could be found and treated early too.

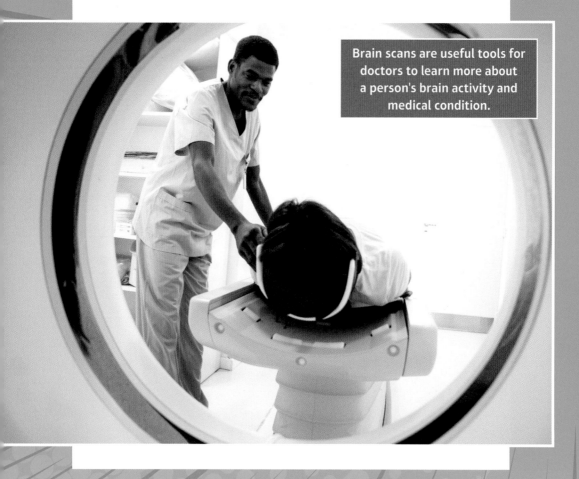

Brain scans are useful tools for doctors to learn more about a person's brain activity and medical condition.

Looking at many scans over a long period of time helps doctors see if our brains are healing or getting worse after an injury. Those same machines can help track how our brains age and alert us to the possibility of memory disorders like Alzheimer's disease or dementia. Getting treatment as soon as possible can help prevent or delay loss of brain function.

Brain scans let doctors see unusual activity or changes that need to be addressed.

Composers can use modern technology to make new music. They wear caps called brain composers that measure brain waves. The wearer thinks of a song, and the cap collects brain waves and turns them into simple music. A similar device can help people open locks with their minds. The user thinks of numbers in a passcode. If the numbers are correct, the lock opens.

Some technologists imagine a world in which things like keyboards, touchscreens, and steering wheels aren't needed anymore. Controlling technology with your mind could be quicker, easier, and more secure.

Caps connected to computers can monitor electrical activity in the brain.

Mind-reading technology could help doctors better understand why someone is experiencing depression and how to help them.

SUPERFAST FACT

Depression and attention disorders affect people of all ages. Millions of people suffer from one or both conditions.

The medical field is developing new, incredible ways to use mind-control devices. Sometimes, a person's mind is healthy but their body needs help to survive. Their lives can be made easier with the latest medical technology.

Brain-chip technology lets paralyzed people who can't talk control computers with their minds. They can use this technology to communicate their needs. One day, they might be able to have their thoughts turned into text, allowing them to communicate directly with loved ones again. They could also control their wheelchairs with their minds.

The future of mind control may start with artificial body parts.

SUPER STEM BREAKTHROUGH

Patients use artificial devices called prosthetics to replace missing limbs. Traditionally, prosthetics were strapped to the wearer's body. The body's movement controlled the limb. But bionic limbs read signals from the person's muscles. They can also react to electrical signals from the brain and nerves. Because the prosthetics are communicating with the brain the way muscles do, the person can use their mind to control the prosthesis the same way they would move a natural limb.

CHAPTER 4

CONTROLLING THE FUTURE

Technology companies are developing new ways to allow technology and human thoughts to merge seamlessly.

Giant tech companies are thinking about how our brains work. They are spending a lot of money to create new mind-control technology. What was once just imagined in comic books and movies is becoming closer to reality.

One technology company is making a special wristband. It will let people control their phones and computers with their brains. It decodes electrical signals from the brain and figures out what the wearer wants to do. People won't have to touch anything. One thought, and they could write a message, click a link, or share a photo.

In the future, you may be able to just think a text message instead of typing it.

Other technology companies are creating brain-computer interfaces. They use special threads that can be implanted in the brain. One day, the threads might allow you to control your smartphone or computer with your thoughts!

Special threads implanted in the brain may help us interact with technology using thoughts.

An adult brain weighs around 3 pounds (1.4 kg). It uses about 20 percent of the body's energy.

The adult brain is typically about 2 percent of a human's body weight.

In the future, you could play a video game without having to touch a controller. Instead of pressing a combination of buttons to perform an action, a simple thought will do. Players who might not have the physical ability to hold a controller or click a mouse could finally get the chance to play on a level playing field with others. This will make video games more inclusive for everyone.

Soldiers one day might control drones with their minds.

The United States Army is trying to create weapons that are controlled by the brain. Soldiers operate drones by remote control. They use cameras mounted on the drones to see where they are going. But drones controlled by pilots' minds could fly better and respond faster.

Mind control is more than a superpower. Paired with technology, it has the potential to make a positive impact on everyone. It will change the way we interact with others. It could make it quicker to communicate or make gaming available to everyone. It might even improve the lives of sick and injured people. The possibilities are exciting to dream about!

SUPER YOU!

Want to try a really cool magic trick that plays tricks on your brain? Make a rubber pencil! Your friends won't believe their eyes. Here's how to make this trick real.

Hold the pencil by its eraser between your thumb and forefinger. Wiggle it up and down. Play with different speeds until it wobbles like rubber. Show off your new trick. Do your friends think it's a real rubber pencil?

GLOSSARY

brainwash: to change a person's beliefs through mind control techniques

depression: a mental health disorder that interferes with a person's daily life

disorder: an illness or issue that disrupts a person's normal physical or mental abilities

gesture: a hand or body movement to express an idea or meaning

hypnotism: the act of putting someone in a hypnotic trance

parasite: an organism that lives in or on an animal of another species and uses that animal to get food, grow, or multiply

prosthesis: an artificial body part

tactile: something sensed by touch

therapy: physical or mental treatment of an injury, disease, or disorder

LEARN MORE

Bloom, Molly Hunegs. *Brains On! Presents…It's Alive: From Neurons and Narwhals to the Fungus Among Us.* New York: Little, Brown and Company, 2020.

Drimmer, Stephanie Warren. *Brain Games: Mighty Book of Mind Benders.* Washington, D.C.: National Geographic, 2019.

Easy Science for Kids: Hypnosis
https://easyscienceforkids.com/hypnosis/

Furgang, Kathy. *Using Your Brain.* New York: Enslow Publishing, 2020.

Kiddle: Mind Control
https://kids.kiddle.co/Mind_control

Mindfulness for Kids
https://www.mindful.org/mindfulness-for-kids/

ScienceKids New Zealand–Brain Machine Interface Video
https://www.sciencekids.co.nz/videos/technology/mindcontrol.html

Silverman, Buffy. *Cutting-Edge Brain Science.* Minneapolis: Lerner Publications, 2020.

INDEX

Photo Acknowledgments

Image credits: fpphotobank/Getty Images, p.4; PonyWang/Getty Images,
p.5; feedough/Getty Images, p.6; bymuratdeniz/Getty Images, p.7; SvetaZi/
Shutterstock, p.8; Jon Feingersh Photography Inc/Getty Images, p.9; delcarmat/
Shutterstock, p.10; Danomyte/Shutterstock, p.11; Digital Storm/Shutterstock,
p.12; Marc Romanelli/Getty Images, p.13; D-Keine/Getty Images, p.14; Tim Platt/
Getty Images, p.15; Philippe TURPIN/Getty Images, p.16; South_agency/Getty
Images, p.17; Hispanolistic/Getty Images, p.18; Monty Rakusen/Getty Images,
p.19; William Taufic/Getty Images, p.20; PeopleImages/Getty Images, p.21; Mark
Runnacles/Stringer/Getty Images, p.22; Brandi Simons/Stringer/Getty Images,
p.23; Jakarin2521/Getty Images, p.24; Carlo A/Getty Images, p.25; Just_Super/
Getty Images, p.26; Dimitri Otis/Getty Images, p.27; John Moore / Staff/Getty
Images, p.28; Sebastian Condrea/Getty Images, p.29;

Cover: eranicle/Getty Images